EXPERIMENT WITH
MAGNETISM
AND ELECTRICITY

Written by Margaret Whalley

Science Consultant: Dr. Christine Sutton
Nuclear Physics Department, University of Oxford

Education Consultant: Ruth Bessant

PRINCETON ■ LONDON

www.two-canpublishing.com

Published in the United States and Canada by
Two-Can Publishing LLC
234 Nassau Street
Princeton, NJ 08542

For information on Two-Can books and multimedia,
call 1-609-921-6700, fax 1-609-921-3349, or visit our Web site at
http://www.two-canpublishing.com

Author: Bryan Murphy
Illustrator: Nancy Anderson
Designer: Linda Blakemore
Science Consultant: Dr. Christine Sutton
Education Consultant: Ruth Bessant

hc ISBN 1-58728-243-7
sc ISBN 1-58728-115-5

hc 1 2 3 4 5 6 7 8 9 10 02
sc 1 2 3 4 5 6 7 8 9 10 02

All photographs are by Paul Bricknell, except for the following: p. 7 (bottom right),
Science Photo Library/ Alex Bartel; p. 8 (top right), Ann Ronan; p. 9 (bottom right),
ZEFA/ Johnny Johnson; p. 16 (bottom left), ZEFA/ John Flowerdrew; p. 17 (top right),
Science Photo Library/ David Parker; p. 19 (center right), Oxford Scientific Films/ Warren Faidley;
p. 28 (top right), Science Photo Library/ Sinclair Stammers; p. 28 (bottom left), ZEFA/
T. Braise; p. 29 (center right), Science Photo Library/ European Space Agency.

Thanks to the staff and pupils of St. George's School, Hanover Square, London.
Thanks also to Siobhán Power.

Printed in Hong Kong by Wing King Tong

CONTENTS

WHAT ARE MAGNETS?

Have you ever used a magnet? Maybe you have a magnet holding notes or drawings to your refrigerator. A magnet is usually a piece of metal that **attracts** or pulls other metal objects toward it. The power to attract metal is called **magnetism.**

▶ Most magnets are made from iron or another metal that contains iron. Magnets come in many shapes and sizes. They can be shaped like horseshoes, bars, rings, or cylinders.

◀ Hikers use **magnetic compasses** to find their way through the wilderness. The needle of the compass is a magnet. The needle always points north because it is pulled by the magnetism of the earth. The earth's magnetism is greatest near the North Pole.

Never put a magnet near electrical appliances—it may damage the magnetic parts inside.

Many household appliances, such as washing machines, radios, and vacuum cleaners, need magnets to work. Computer monitors use magnets to display images on the screen. A computer's **floppy disks** store information with the help of magnetic material.

Look around and collect objects that you think a magnet might pick up. Then test them with a magnet. You can buy magnets at toy stores or hobby shops.

PUSH OR PULL

Every magnet has two areas called **poles**, where the magnet's pull feels the strongest. On a bar magnet, the poles are usually at opposite ends. Find the poles on your magnet. How many pins can you hang from different places on the magnet?

▲ Push the ends of two magnets together. Do their poles attract each other? Do they **repel**, or push apart? Try turning one of the magnets around. Now what happens?

The two poles of a magnet are called either "north" or "south." When you try to put two like poles together, they repel each other. Unlike poles, one north and one south, will attract each other.

▶ Tape small magnets on the backs of some toy trains or cars. Some will repel and race away from each other.

6

Try this experiment to see how a magnet can seem to "float" in the air. Use two magnets of the same shape—round or bar-shaped work best. Find the areas on the magnets that repel each other and mark these poles with a marker or paint. Push one magnet into a thick pad of modeling clay with the marked pole facing up. Stick several pencils or crayons around it to make a strong fence. Now lower the second magnet above the first with its marked pole facing down. What happens to the top magnet? Push it down gently with your finger. What do you feel? Can you force the magnets together?

▲ This modern train has no wheels. The train is called a maglev—short for magnetic levitation, which means it has the ability to float on magnetism. Just like the magnets in the experiment above, the magnets under the train and on top of the rail repel each other.

7

NORTH AND SOUTH

People have used magnetic compasses for many centuries to help them find their way over land, on the sea, and in the air. The very first compasses were probably pieces of magnetic stone called **lodestone**. People discovered long ago that when this stone was allowed to hang freely, it always pointed north.

▼ Find out which end of your bar magnet will point to the north. Fill two glasses with sand and place a long stick across them. Hang a bar magnet from the stick with string. Use a compass to check which way the magnet points. Now you can label the north-seeking pole "north" and the other pole "south."

▲ Greek legend tells of a shepherd from a place called Magnesia. His metal shepherd's crook stuck to a large, lodestone rock. The Greeks named these stones "magnets" after the shepherd's birthplace.

Scientists have discovered that the earth itself acts like a huge magnet. One pole, called the **magnetic north pole**, appears to be in the far north. The **magnetic south pole** lies in the far south. The north pole of an ordinary magnet or compass needle is attracted to the earth's magnetic north pole. These magnetic poles are not located in the same spots as the North Pole and South Pole, which are names given to the northernmost and southernmost places on the earth's surface.

You can make your own compass the way early scientists did. Magnetize a needle by stroking it across one pole of a magnet 50 times in the same direction. Tape the magnetized needle to the top of a flat cork. Float the cork in a bowl of water. Now watch as the cork and needle swing to point in one direction. Use a magnetic compass to check which end of the needle is pointing north. Now you can label the cork with the north and south poles of the needle.

The earth's magnetism traps tiny particles that travel to earth from the sun. These particles drift close to the earth's magnetic north and south poles. As they collide with particles in the air near the poles, the sky begins to glow and a strange curtain of light appears. The ghostly, dancing lights are known as the **aurora,** or the northern and southern lights.

MAGNETIC ATTRACTION

Can a magnet's power work through different materials? Using your magnet, try picking up a pin through thin pieces of cloth, paper, plastic, or rubber. Is the magnet's pull weaker? Which material causes the most change to your magnet's pull?

▶ Have a magnetic fishing contest. Cut some fish shapes out of brightly colored paper and slide a paper clip onto each one. Put the fish in a large bowl. Tie a magnet to the end of a string on a stick. Can you also catch fish through the side of the bowl?

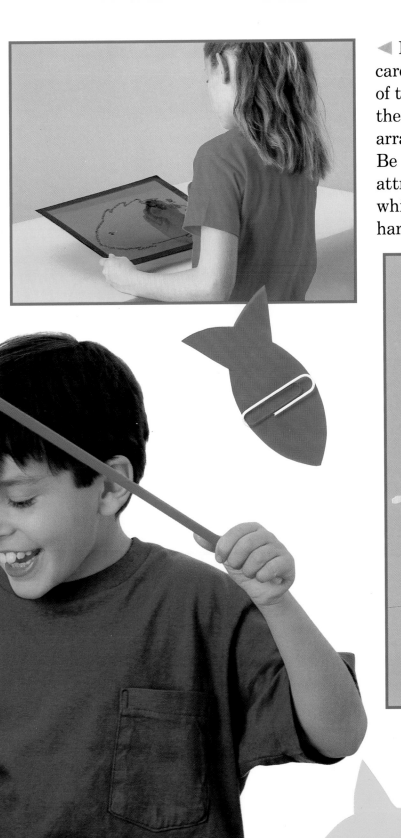

Draw a hairy creature on a firm sheet of cardboard or plastic. With small pins on top of the sheet, move a strong magnet under the board. Use the force of the magnet to arrange the pins as the creature's hair. Be sure to use pins that you know will be attracted to a magnet. (Or use iron filings, which are available in hobby shops and hardware stores.)

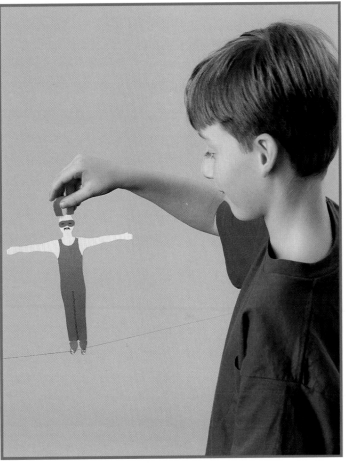

Make a paper acrobat. Tape a sewing needle to the figure's back and paper clips to its feet. Feed some thread through the paper clips, then stretch the thread taut between two chairs. Find the position where a magnet can keep the acrobat dancing upright on its high wire.

MAKE OR BREAK

A magnet's power to attract or repel can damage the magnetism in electrical appliances.

▶ Magnets can harm audio or video equipment. See for yourself by dragging a magnet over an unwanted audiocassette tape. Now play the tape. The magnet has upset the magnetic sound pattern on the tape ribbon.

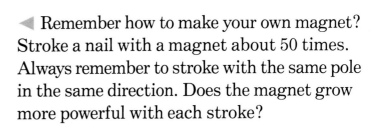

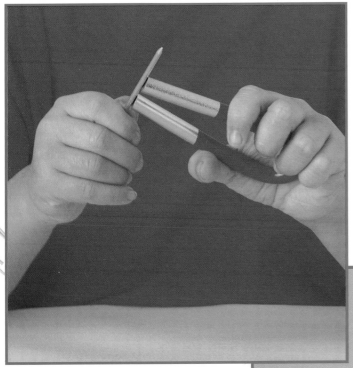

◀ Remember how to make your own magnet? Stroke a nail with a magnet about 50 times. Always remember to stroke with the same pole in the same direction. Does the magnet grow more powerful with each stroke?

◀ You can make long chains of paper clips with a strong magnet. Each clip attracts the next. Does the chain lose its magnetism if you pull it off the magnet?

▶ Even though a magnet seems strong, its powers can often be taken away. Write down how many pins your magnetized nail can pick up. Tap the nail on the edge of a table five times. How many pins will it pick up now? Repeat the tapping until the nail no longer attracts the pins. Rough handling can make a magnet weaker.

FIELDS OF FORCE

The magnet's power to push and pull exists only in an area called the **magnetic field.** A magnet cannot attract or repel an object that is outside this field.

Here is a way to see this field. Label two bar magnets with their north and south poles. (Use the experiment on page 8.) Place the two magnets side by side under a sheet of paper, with their north poles facing the same way. Sprinkle iron filings on the paper. Tap the sheet gently.

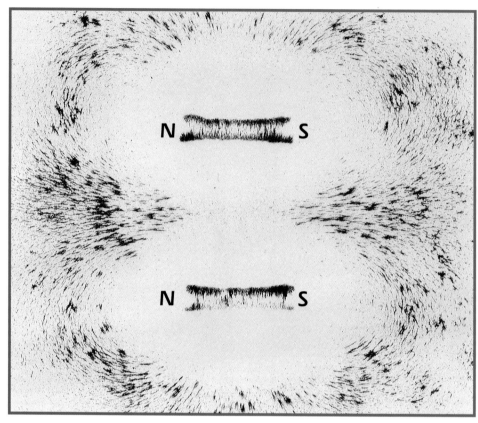

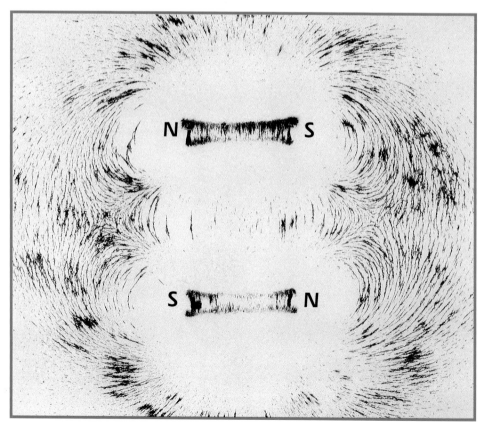

The filings arrange themselves in a pattern of curved lines and straight spokes. The lines traced by the filings show where the magnets' **lines of force** are.

Repeat the experiment, this time with the north pole of one magnet facing the same way as the south pole of the other magnet. Do not let the magnets touch. How has the magnetic field changed?

Migrating birds use the sun and stars to help them find their way. On cloudy days, you would expect them to be confused and off course, but they are not. Some scientists believe that the birds have a magnetic sense and use the earth's magnetic field as a guide.

A horseshoe magnet usually has a **keeper,** in the shape of a small metal bar, to stop its ability to attract. Line up some paper clips in front of a horseshoe magnet. Find the point at which they are attracted. Now put the keeper on the magnet and try again. How does the keeper change the magnetic field around the magnet? Can you find other materials that change the power of a horseshoe magnet?

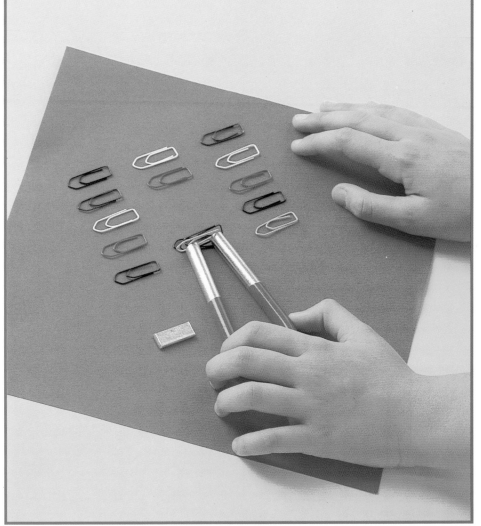

POWER BASE

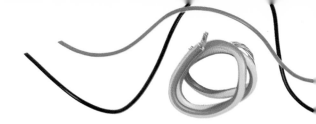

Electricity, a form of energy that can produce heat, light, or power, is caused by the actions of tiny bits of matter called atoms. Atoms are made up of even smaller particles. Of these, the **electrons** create electricity with the negative charges they carry. The flow of these electrons through wires produces most of the electricity we use every day.

▶ How many uses of electricity can you find in your home?

Electricity helps people at home and at work. In factories, forklift trucks lift heavy loads, and robots build cars. Electric furnaces melt metals and bake clay into bricks. In offices, fax machines, photocopiers, and computers save the time and effort of many workers.

◀ An amusement park ride needs electricity to spin its riders. Most forms of transportation now use electricity. Electric trains and buses carry people in cities. Ships and airplanes are steered with the help of electronic instruments.

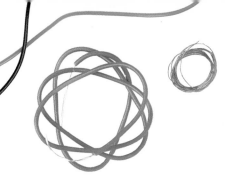

▶ A city never shuts down for the night. In the evening, many people go out to theaters, eat in restaurants, or attend lighted football games. Traffic moves through the city, and the streetlights shine all night. Without electricity, much of this activity would stop at sundown.

◀ Electricity occurs in the natural world, too. A fish called the electric eel can produce a jolt of electricity from special organs along the length of its body. The eel uses electricity to defend itself, or to stun or kill prey with an electric shock. An eel can produce about 500 **volts** of electrical energy, which is enough to stun a large animal. Electric eels also use their electricity to guide them through the murky water at the bottom of a river. The electricity helps the eels sense and avoid objects around them.

FANTASTIC STATIC

In dry air, you can make a kind of electricity just by rubbing. Rubbing makes **static electricity**, an arrangement of electrons that do not move. Although they are "static," these charged particles have the power to attract like magnets.

▼ Rub a balloon on your wool sweater, then hold the balloon over your head. The balloon is now surrounded by a charged area of electrons called an **electric field**, where the electrons have the power to pull light objects. It's hair-raising!

Charge a balloon with static electricity by rubbing it against your sweater, then hold it next to a thin stream of dripping water. Like magic, the water bends toward the balloon. The electric field around the balloon pulls things toward it. How far can you make the stream bend?

Make paper bugs and put them in a shallow box with a clear plastic lid. Rub the lid with a dust cloth to create a static charge. The bugs will jump up and stick to the lid. Move your finger over the lid to make the bugs dance.

With the rapid rubbing of water particles, static electricity builds up inside growing thunderclouds. Lightning is a giant electrical spark caused when this static charge is released suddenly. In a flash, this spark can jump inside clouds, between clouds, or from a cloud down to earth.

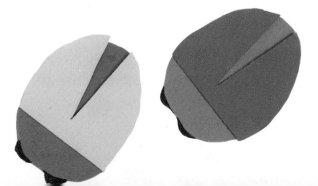

LET IT FLOW

The electricity we use for power is not static electricity but **current electricity**. This type of electricity is made up of electrons flowing from place to place. To picture the movement of electrons through wire, think of beads flowing through a tube. This movement of electrons creates the flow of electricity, or the **electric current**. The wire allows electricity to flow to where it is needed.

In 1820 a Danish professor named Hans Christian Ørsted was giving a lecture. He dropped a live electric wire across a magnetic compass. As he picked up the wire, he noticed that the compass needle had swung out of place and was no longer pointing north. Ørsted was the first person to notice that wires carrying electricity have a magnetic field.

◀ Later in that century, a famous scientist named Michael Faraday found that if he moved a magnet in and out of a coil of wire, an electric current would flow through the wire. He could now **generate**, or produce, electricity.

▶ Did you know that **batteries** were invented about 200 years ago? They come in all shapes and sizes, from tiny batteries for watches to large ones for cars and trucks.

◀ You can make a battery with an iron key or washer, a copper penny, sandpaper, a paper towel, vinegar, and wire. Rub the coin and the key or washer with sandpaper. Dip a small square of the paper towel in vinegar and place it between the coin and the key or washer. Wrap the wire 10 times around a magnetic compass. Hold one exposed end of the wire to the washer or key. Hold the other exposed end to the coin. The electric current in the wire will make the compass needle move.

▶ Batteries store chemicals that react together to push electrons along a wire and create electrical power. When the chemicals are used up, the battery becomes "dead." Which of your toys use batteries?

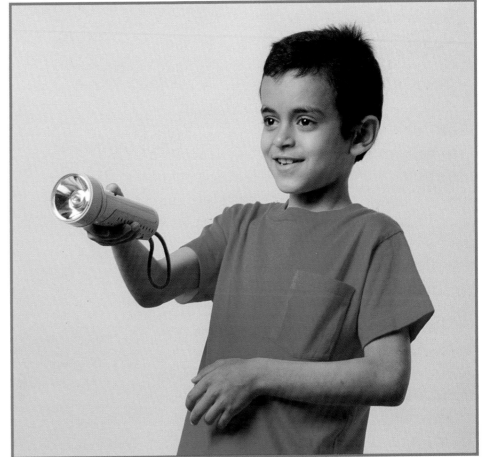

LIGHTING UP

two bulb holders

plastic-coated stranded wire

Never try these experiments using the electric outlets at home. The amount of electricity flowing through a building's electrical system is very high and very dangerous.

Before attaching wires to bulb holders or batteries, ask an adult to help you remove the plastic coating from the ends of the wire. Use a sharp scissors or knife to cut through only the plastic, leaving about ½ inch of exposed wire.

two 2.5v or 3.5v flashlight bulbs with screw fittings

alligator clips

bell wire

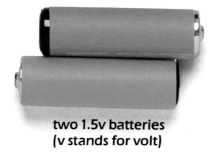

two 1.5v batteries (v stands for volt)

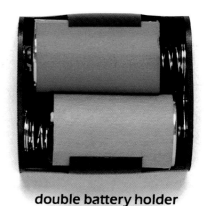

double battery holder

To harness electricity, we need to create a closed path or **circuit** where electricity can flow. Connecting a wire from each **terminal** (metal end) on a battery to a bulb holder will make a circuit and light the bulb. You can buy all the items to make circuits from an electronics supply store or hobby shop.

▶ Make your own simple circuit. Insert a flashlight bulb in a bulb holder. Use electrician's tape to attach the bell wire from the holder, one to each end of a single battery. Is there a difference in the bulb's light if you switch the wires on the terminals of the battery?

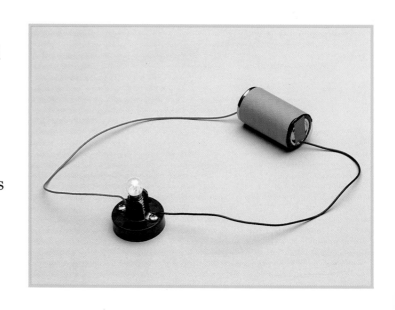

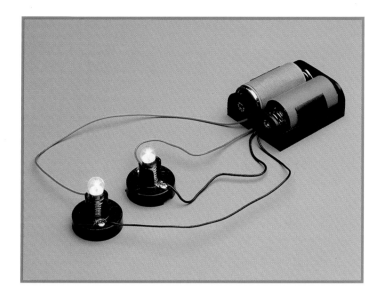

Was there a change in the brightness of the bulbs when you tried the two different kinds of circuits? What difference would it make if you used only one battery in each circuit?

▼ Make a light-up frog. Draw a frog on one side of some folded cardboard. Use a pencil to make two holes in the cardboard where the eyes should be. Tuck the circuit with two bulb holders and the battery holder in back of the frog. Push the bulbs through the holes in the cardboard. Ask an adult to make holes in two Ping-Pong balls, then place them over the bulbs. Connect the wires from the bulb holders to the battery holder and watch the eyes light up!

▲ Put two batteries in a battery holder. Each battery must be placed in the holder the right way for electricity to flow. Use bell wires to join each of two bulbs directly to the battery holder as shown above. Try unscrewing one bulb. What happens to the remaining bulb? Can you guess why?

▼ Now make a circuit in which only one loop of bell wire connects two bulbs with each other and the battery holder terminals. Both bulbs are on one circuit. What happens to this circuit if you unscrew a bulb?

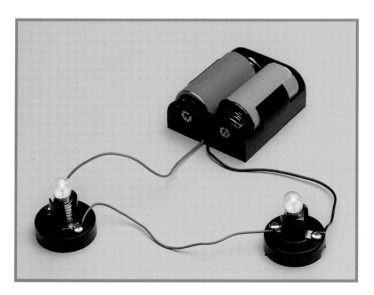

CONDUCTORS

Materials that let electric current flow through them, such as wires, are known as **conductors**. Electricity cannot pass through other materials called **insulators**. Insulators, like the plastic coating around electric wires, stop currents from flowing where they could be dangerous.

To make a switch for your bulb, wrap two cardboard strips in foil. Clip the strips into a circuit. Touch the strips together and the bulb lights up. Each time you separate the strips, you break the circuit and stop the flow of electricity. In the same way, each time you turn off a light, you break a circuit. Turn it on, and the circuit is complete again.

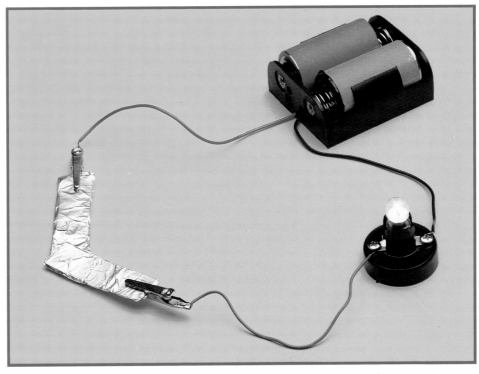

What other materials conduct electricity? To find out, remove the cardboard strips from the clips in the above circuit. Put different objects between the clips. The current is flowing if the bulb lights up. Are any of your selected items conductors?

Some burglar alarms turn on when a person steps on part of a security system. The pressure closes a circuit, and may trigger an alarm bell, flashing lights, and even an alarm at the local police station.

ELECTROMAGNETS

In its basic form, an **electromagnet** is a coil of wire with an iron bar through it. The bar instantly becomes a magnet when an electric current flows through the wire. The flow of electrons through the wire creates a magnetic field around the iron.

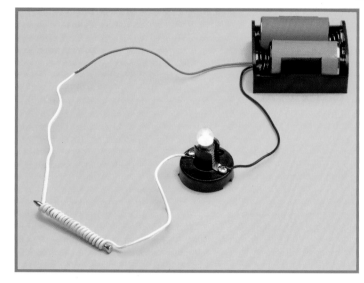

▲ To make an electromagnet, set up a circuit using stranded wire wrapped many times very closely and tightly around an iron nail. Connect the stranded wire to a battery holder. Include a bulb in the circuit to keep the wire from getting hot. How many paper clips can your electromagnet lift? Change the strength of the magnet by winding more wire around the nail or by using a different number of batteries.

▲ Huge electromagnets are used to pick out magnetic metals for recycling from piles of scrap. A crane lifts the electromagnet and any metal stuck to it. When the electric current is cut off, the electromagnet drops its load.

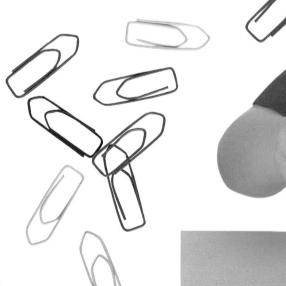

Make an electromagnetic truck. Fold a cardboard strip to make the arm of the crane. Glue in a large thread spool at one end. Cut slits at one end of a box and insert the crane's arms through the slits, with the spool end in the truck. Push a pencil in one side of the box, through the spool, and out the other side of the box.

Wind the center portion of stranded wire around a nail about 30 times. Thread the loose ends of the wire through the free end of the crane, down the arms, and around the spool. In front of the spool, connect the wire ends to a bulb holder and battery placed inside the truck. What can your truck pick up? To save the battery, disconnect the wires when you are not using the truck.

POWER SOURCES

The electricity we use every day is produced in power plants. Most plants burn coal, gas, or oil, or use nuclear fuels to make steam.

Coal heats water to make steam. The steam then spins the blades of a machine called a **turbine**, which generates the electricity. Afterward, the steam is cooled to become water again.

▶ These huge towers cool the steam at a coal-burning power plant.

From a power plant, electricity travels on a network of thick wires. In towns and cities, the electricity flows through both overhead and underground **cables**, which are large, insulated wires.

Burning fuels can pollute the earth's atmosphere. Scientists and engineers have been working on finding cleaner ways to produce electricity. One way is to use the force of falling water to spin turbines. This kind of power is called **hydroelectricity**.

◀ The wind spins the blades of these large windmills—just like your breath spins a toy pinwheel—and generates electricity with the power of moving air.

Another way to produce electricity is to use sunlight. Solar cells are thin layers of hard, shiny material that can change rays of light into electricity. Large panels of solar cells use the sun's energy to power satellites that orbit the earth.

GLOSSARY

attract: to make something come closer. Magnets can easily attract objects made of iron.

aurora: streaks of light near the earth's magnetic poles. They are created by a clash of charged particles from the sun with the earth's atmosphere. Auroras are also known as the northern and southern lights.

battery: a container of stored chemicals that react together to make electricity

cables: heavy, thick, insulated wires used to carry electricity from place to place

circuit: a closed path traveled by an electric current. A gap in a circuit breaks the path so the current no longer flows.

conductors: materials through which electricity is able to flow

current electricity: the movement of electrons from place to place

electric current: the flow of electrons through a wire or other conductor

electric field: the area around an electrically charged object, such as a balloon, where it has the power to attract or repel

electricity: a form of energy used to make light, heat, and power to run machinery

electromagnet: a coil of wire around an iron bar, which acts as a magnet when electric current flows through the wire

electrons: tiny charged particles that form electricity

floppy disks: plastic sheets coated with magnetic material on which computer information can be stored

generate: to create or produce something. Machines that produce electricity are called generators.

hydroelectricity: a type of power that uses falling water to generate electricity

insulators: materials that stop the flow of electric current from going to the wrong places. Electricity cannot easily flow through materials that are insulators.

keeper: a small piece of metal that stops a horseshoe magnet from attracting things when the magnet is not in use and that protects the magnetic power of the magnet

lines of force: the patterns that magnetic force forms around a magnet. These lines indicate the direction that the magnetic force is pulling or pushing.

lodestone: an iron-containing rock that is a natural magnet

magnetic compass: a device that has a moving needle that always points north.

magnetic field: the area around a magnet where its magnetic force, or its power, to attract or repel exists

magnetic north pole and **magnetic south pole:** locations within the earth where its magnetism is the strongest

magnetism: the pulling force of a magnet on things made of iron

poles: the places on a magnet where the magnetic effect is strongest. Every magnet has two poles.

repel: to push away

solar cells: thin layers of a hard, shiny material that can change sunlight into electricity

static electricity: nonmoving charged electrons, produced when some materials are rubbed together

terminal: one metal end of a battery. Each battery has two terminals. A circuit must run between them for electricity to flow.

turbine: a large machine or fan that is turned by steam, running water, wind, or gas. It spins a magnet inside coiled wire to make electricity.

volt: a measurement of electrical force

INDEX